# MEMORY LANGUAGE

How to develop powerful recall in 48 minutes

To B Laville —

Best wishes

ALLAN PEASE
BARBARA PEASE

# MEMORY LANGUAGE

## How to develop powerful recall in 48 minutes

Illustrated by Karen Barbouttis

Pease Learning Systems Pty Ltd
Sydney, Australia

*Reprinted 1994*

*First published November 1992 by*
*Pease Learning Systems, Phone (02) 973 1150, Fax (02) 973 1169*
*PO Box 12, Mona Vale, 2103, NSW, Australia.*
*ISBN 0 646 1206111 1*
*Edited and designed by Murray Child & Company, Phone (02) 971 0067*
*Illustrated by Karen Barbouttis, Fax (02) 362 4137*
*Cover designed by Sue Irvine, Fax (02) 362 4137*
*Cover concept by Ian Coles*
*Cover photographs by Clifford White Photography, Phone (02) 982 6363*
*Printed by Australian Print Group, Maryborough, Victoria*

*Distributors:*
*Australia and New Zealand: Harper Collins Publishers*
*Pease Learning Systems, (hard cover edition).*
*Asia—Reed International*

For
Jasmine, Adam,
Bill and Ray

***Acknowledgements***

We thank the following people for their advice and contributions to this book: Jack Collis, Ray and Ruth Pease, the McCameys, Sue Irvine, Peter Draper, Karen Barbouttis, Carolyn and Murray Child.

# Introduction

No single mental ability is more important to personal success than a powerful memory.

While most adults and children have the capacity for phenomenal memory, few ever know the simple secrets of harnessing this amazing ability.

Learning the techniques in MEMORY LANGUAGE and practising often is the key to powerful memory recall.

This book is written in a simple, easy-to-read style and the cartoon format and humorous stories will enable everyone to learn while being amused and entertained. It will teach both children and adults the valuable skill of imagery. You should be able to master the basic technique in less than an hour—the average adult reader can do it in 48 minutes!

AT THE END OF THIS BOOK YOU WILL BE **AMAZED** AT THE RECALL ABILITY THAT YOU AND YOUR CHILDREN HAVE DEVELOPED.

To get the best out of this book follow these simple guidelines:

- It is important that each reader knows the nursery rhyme song in the book. If you don't know it, turn to page 35 and practise it before you begin the story.
- The story is about two children who are asked to take a trip to the shops and remember a list of ten items. In reality, you would not ask young children to remember such a large list and the average adult would have difficulty remembering half this number of items. But in this book it is an essential part of the story to teach the lessons.
- We will be asking the readers to clearly visualise a number of images known as **Memory Pegs**. Each person may imagine a different

version of them. For example, if you ask eight-year-olds to visualise a shoe one child may think of a ballet shoe, another might see a football boot and an adult could picture a sneaker. It is important to let each reader have his or her own version of the **Memory Peg** because personalisation makes recall easier.

• This is a participation book so get **everyone** involved. When the children in the story begin to visualise their Grandfather's instructions, stop the story and you and your children do the **same** exercise. Study each illustration and ask everyone to comment on it. Then ask them to recall the item they think belongs to that page.

And when you've all mastered the skills, let the kids use the book as a colouring book. Most of all, have a good time.

ALLAN PEASE
BARBARA PEASE

# MEMORY
# LANGUAGE

Adam was sad.

His Mother's birthday was today and he and his sister Jasmine had decided to make a special gift for her.

Jasmine had made a beautiful, coloured paper flower and Adam should have painted patterns all around the flowerpot in which it sat.

But Adam had forgotten to do his part!

Adam felt that his mother would think that he didn't care about her.

And Jasmine was angry with him.

All because he had a bad memory.

"If I'd remembered to paint the flowerpot, Mum would have her birthday present and Jasmine wouldn't be angry with me," he thought.

BUS
STOP
?

The next morning the kids caught the school bus, as usual.

But now Jasmine had a feeling that **she** had forgotten something.

What was it?

“Good morning, children,” said the teacher.

“Good morning, Mrs Varney,” replied the children.

“Please hand in the notes from your parents allowing you to go on the class beach trip today,” she said.

**Now** Jasmine knew what she had forgotten!

It was **her** responsibility to bring the beach note to the teacher so that she and Adam could also go to the beach with the class.

But she had forgotten it!

"Adam and Jasmine, because you don't have your note you won't be able to come to the beach with us today. You'll have to spend the day studying in the school library," said Mrs Varney.

"If only I had remembered!" thought Jasmine. "Adam and I would be having a great day at the beach with our friends."

"I wish I had a good memory," she said.

YOU'LL HAVE TO SPEND THE DAY STUDYING IN THE SCHOOL LIBRARY !!

LIBRARY
KB©

The class waved goodbye to the kids and headed for the beach.

After school Adam and Jasmine had to walk all the way home. The school bus was at the beach with the class.

They didn't even want to go out and play.

All the other kids would be talking about was what a fun day they'd had swimming and building sand castles.

At the bus stop the next morning their friend James was very upset with them.

“Where were you both yesterday?” asked James. “We had a great time at my birthday party, but you two weren’t there. Why didn’t you come?”

“Gee, James, we’re sorry. We forgot. Bad Memory again!” said the kids.

BAD MEMORY AGAIN!!
BUS STOP

Before bed that night Jasmine and Adam discussed their memory problem.

"What can we do about our forgetfulness?" asked Adam.

"First I forgot to paint Mum's flowerpot, then you left our school note at home and now we've both forgotten James' birthday party!"

"What are we going to do?" sighed Jasmine. "Who knows the answer?"

"Grandpa!" they both cried.

GRANDPA!

The next day after school they went to see Grandpa.

“Grandpa, we have a problem. We forget things all the time.”

Grandpa smiled.

“What can we do?” they asked.

“Well...” said Grandpa, “I have a special trick that will help you to remember almost anything.”

“In fact, remembering is **easy** when you know how.”

“Remembering is not easy for **us,** Grandpa,” said the kids.

“We’re always forgetting to do things.”

Grandpa laughed.

“No, kids. You just haven’t learned how to use your memory the way it was meant to be used.”

The kids’ eyes lit up. Was there a way that they could learn how to remember things?

“I’ll explain,” said Grandpa.

FUN FOTOS
MATHS
ENGLISH

"Let's say that on Sunday morning your Mother gives you a list of ten things to do before lunch. She says,

children, I want you to

1. **feed the cat** and
2. **pick up your toys.** Then you can buy an
3. **ice-cream cone** each from the shop. Also buy
4. **a big tomato** for sandwiches. Then go to the supermarket and buy
5. **a custard pie** for dessert and
6. **a dozen eggs.** On the way home, pick up our
7. **holiday photos** from the chemist and then get the
8. **chocolate cake** that Mrs Suter has baked for us. When you get back I want you to
9. **water the garden** and then
10. **do your homework.**

When you've finished, we'll have lunch."

“Now that’s a lot to remember, isn’t it?” said Grandpa.

“How could **anyone** remember all that?” sighed Jasmine.

“Well, I’m going to teach you the **secret** of how to do it!” whispered Grandpa. “The secret is…

**MEMORY PEGS and SILLY STORIES.**”

The children looked blankly at him. What did he mean?

“First you learn **ten memory pegs**,” said Grandpa.

“What’s that?” asked Adam.

“**Pegs** are places to hang things,” said Grandpa.

“You mean like the pegs at school where we hang our school bags?” Jasmine asked.

“That’s right,” Grandpa replied.

MEMORY PEGS
AND
SILLY STORIES!!

"Do you know the song that goes like this…

**This old man he played one he played knick knack on my…"**

"Drum!" cried Jasmine.

"Yes, we know that song, Grandpa!" said the kids.

"OK, then let's start by singing the whole song," said Grandpa.

And so they began to sing…

This old man, he played **one,**
He played knick knack on my **drum,**
*With a knick knack paddy whack, give a dog a bone,*
*This old man came rolling home.*

This old man, he played **two,**
He played knick knack on my **shoe,**
*With a knick knack...etc.*

This old man, he played **three,**
He played knick knack on my **tree,**
*With a knick knack...etc.*

This old man, he played **four,**
He played knick knack on my **door,**
*With a knick knack...etc.*

This old man, he played **five,**
He played knick knack on my **hive,**
*With a knick knack...etc.*

This old man, he played **six,**
He played knick knack on my **sticks,**
*With a knick knack...etc.*

This old man, he played **seven,**
He played knick knack up to **heaven,**
*With a knick knack...etc.*

This old man, he played **eight,**
He played knick knack on my **gate,**
*With a knick knack...etc.*

This old man, he played **nine,**
He played knick knack on my **line,**
*With a knick knack...etc.*

This old man, he played **ten,**
He played knick knack on my **hen,**
*With a knick knack...etc.*

"You see, you already **know** the ten memory pegs!" said Grandpa.

"Now, let's say them again."

"Kids, this song is the secret to having a good memory," said Grandpa.

"Now, I want you to close your eyes and imagine what all the memory pegs would look like," he said.

"What do you mean, Grandpa?" they asked.

"Well," said Grandpa, "for number **ONE** which is **DRUM** imagine a drum that you've seen in a musical band.

For number **TWO** imagine your favourite **SHOE**. At **THREE** imagine a **TREE** that you've seen and for number **FOUR** imagine a bedroom **DOOR**. At **FIVE**, which is **HIVE,** imagine a hive full of bees. For **SIX** imagine some **STICKS** from a tree. At number **SEVEN,** which is **HEAVEN**, imagine an angel floating in the clouds and at **EIGHT** picture a **GATE** that you've seen. For **NINE,** which is **LINE**, see a white line down the middle of the road and finally, at **TEN,** imagine a big fat **HEN**!"

"Are you ready to imagine each of those pegs?" he asked.

"We're ready!" they shouted happily.

So they closed their eyes and began to think of what their memory pegs would look like.

"Now let's go through the list of things that your Mother asked you to do," said Grandpa.

"Item number one on your list is **feed the cat**."

"Adam, what's the memory peg for one?" asked Grandpa.

"**One** is **Drum**," replied Adam.

"Right, so at number one let's imagine that your cat Cosmo is walking down the street early in the morning and he's got a drum full of cat food on his back. There's a tap coming out of the drum and he's eating his breakfast from it! And he's banging the drum with his tail and waking up all the neighbours."

"That's silly!" giggled Adam.

"Yes, and the **sillier** we make it, the **easier** it is to remember!" Grandpa said.

"So one is **DRUM—FEED THE CAT**."

QUIET!!
STOP THAT NOISE!!
SHHH!
GRRR!
CAT FOOD

"Number two on the list is **pick up your toys,**" said Grandpa. "What's the peg for two, Jasmine?"

"**Two** is **Shoe**, Grandpa."

"Right, Jasmine. Now think of a silly story about your shoe and your toys," said Grandpa.

"OK," said Jasmine. "Imagine that my toys are driving around in my shoe and I'm running after them and chasing them into the toybox."

"Now that's **really** silly, Grandpa," Adam laughed.

"Exactly, Adam, and silliness is a very important part of remembering things," said Grandpa.

"Remember, the sillier the better."

"Two is **SHOE—PICK UP YOUR TOYS**."

"Now, what is the memory peg for number three?" Grandpa asked.

"I know, Grandpa, **Three** is **Tree**," said Adam.

Grandpa smiled and said, "Right. And the third item on the list is **ice-cream cones**. Think of a silly story about ice-cream and a tree, Adam."

Adam thought for a moment then said, "Imagine that my cat Cosmo and I are sitting under a tree that grows ice-cream and there's ice-cream cones falling all over us. It's all running down my face and Cosmo and I eat it until we nearly burst! Yum yum."

"And you said **my** stories were silly," Jasmine laughed.

"So Three is **TREE—ICE-CREAM CONES**."

“This is fun,” said Adam.

“What are the next two items on the list?” asked Grandpa.

“A **big tomato** and a **custard pie**,” replied Jasmine.

“Jasmine, you peg the tomato at number four and Adam, you peg the custard pie at number five,” said Grandpa.

So Jasmine closed her eyes, grinned cheekily and said,

“**Four** is **Door**. I’m pretending that I open my bed-room door but the handle has changed into a big tomato and it squashes between my fingers and goes all over the carpet.”

“Let’s make it even sillier,” chuckled Grandpa. “The tomato juice runs down the stairs and all over your Dad’s head!”

“Boy, he’d be **mad!**” laughed Adam.

“Four is **DOOR—A BIG TOMATO**.”

"The memory peg for **Five** is **Hive** and the item is a **custard pie**," said Grandpa.
"What can you do with that, Adam?"

"Ah…that's a hard one, Grandpa. I'm not sure," said Adam hesitantly.

So Grandpa said, "Imagine that you've found a bee-hive and you're teasing the bees by throwing custard pies at them. The bees get really angry, fly out of the hive and sting you on the bottom."

"This is great fun," said the kids.

"Five is **HIVE—CUSTARD PIE**."

OUCH!

"OK, kids, we're halfway through our list," said Grandpa. "Let's see how many you can remember."

So the kids began to repeat the list.

| | | |
|---|---|---|
| One | **DRUM** | **FEED THE CAT** |
| Two | **SHOE** | **PICK UP TOYS** |
| Three | **TREE** | **ICE-CREAM CONES** |
| Four | **DOOR** | **A BIG TOMATO** |
| Five | **HIVE** | **A CUSTARD PIE** |

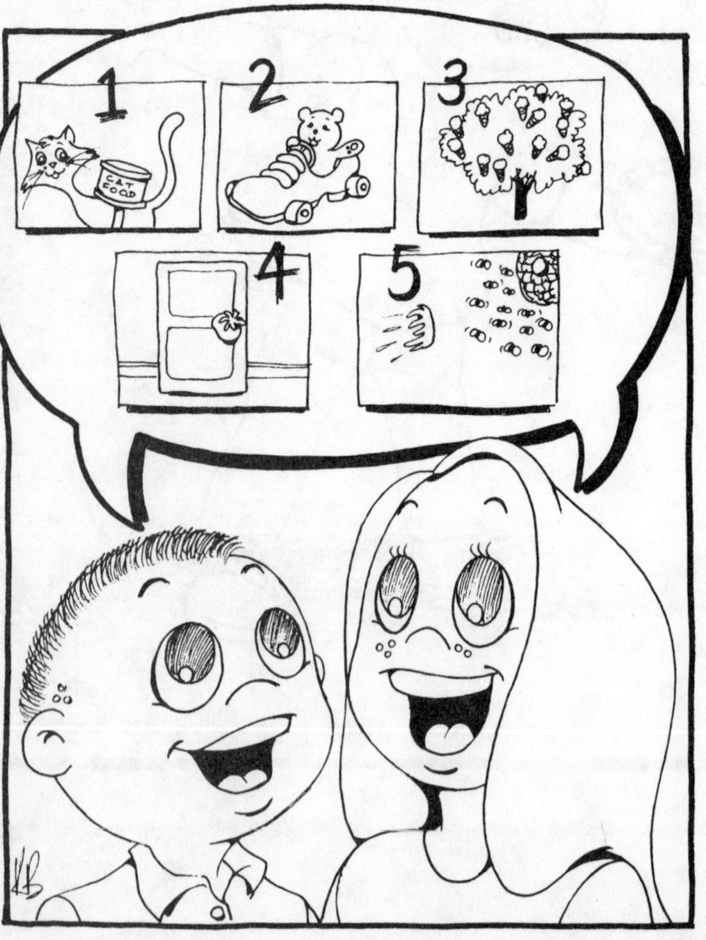

"Great! You've remembered the first five items on the list easily. As you can see, your memories are excellent!" said Grandpa.

Now the kids were becoming really good at making up silly stories and were eager to do the last five.

Grandpa smiled and said, "Jasmine, I want you to peg number six which is **eggs** and number seven which is the **holiday photos**. Adam, you peg number eight which is the **chocolate cake** from Mrs Suter and number nine which is **water the garden**."

"I'll try first," said Jasmine.

"**Six** is **STICKS.** I'm thinking that I'm balancing a dozen eggs on the end of a long stick. It's very difficult because I'm wearing a blindfold and hopping on one foot. Some of the eggs are falling off onto Adam and Cosmo."

"Six is **STICKS—A DOZEN EGGS.**"

"And **Seven** is **Heaven,**" said Jasmine. "Imagine that I'm outside playing and photos of our holidays start falling from heaven. I look up in the sky and there's an angel dropping them down to me. And when I catch a photo I see that it's pictures of us all on holidays and that none of us are wearing any clothes!" she giggled.

"Hmm. . . very well," sighed Grandpa.

"Seven is **HEAVEN—HOLIDAY PHOTOS**. What's next?"

“It’s my turn now,” said Adam.

“My next one is eight, and **Eight** is **GATE**—pick up the **chocolate cake** from Mrs Suter,” said Adam.

“Pretend that I walk past Mrs Suter’s house and she comes out to meet me with the chocolate cake but she falls over the gate and goes head first into the cake! And I try not to laugh.”

“Good. That’s a very silly story,” Grandpa chuckled.

“So Eight is **GATE—CHOCOLATE CAKE**.”

WHEEE!

"What's at number nine?"
"When we get home we're going to **water the garden** and that's at **Nine** which is **LINE**," said Adam.

"Pretend that I'm sitting on a big hose and riding it like a snake in and out of the line down the middle of the road. It's going up and down like a roller coaster and watering all the flowers on the side of the road," he laughed. "It's great fun!"

"So Nine is **LINE—WATER THE GARDEN**."

“Finally we have item number ten, **do your homework**,” said Grandpa.

“And **Ten** is **HEN**,” said Jasmine.

“What’s a good story about a hen and homework?” Grandpa asked.

“Here’s a good one!” said Adam. “We go to the desk where we do our homework and there’s a big fat hen sitting on our school books…”

“…and it’s pecking and scratching at all the pages!” said Jasmine excitedly.

“…and the pages are flying everywhere!” laughed Grandpa.

“So Ten is **HEN—DO YOUR HOMEWORK**.”

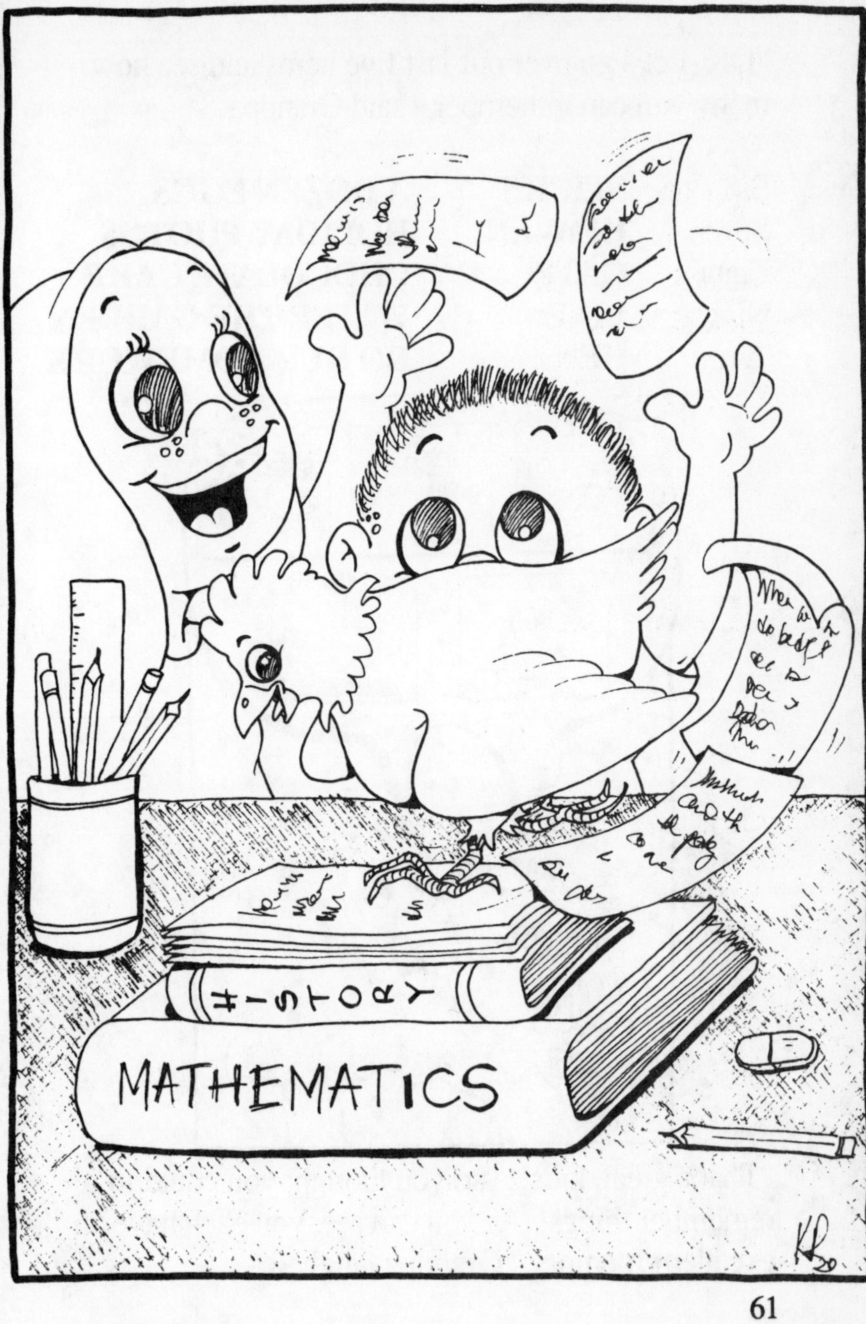
HISTORY
MATHEMATICS

"OK. Let's go over our last five items and see how many you can remember," said Grandpa.

| | | |
|---|---|---|
| Six | **STICKS** | **A DOZEN EGGS** |
| Seven | **HEAVEN** | **HOLIDAY PHOTOS** |
| Eight | **GATE** | **CHOCOLATE CAKE** |
| Nine | **LINE** | **WATER THE GARDEN** |
| Ten | **HEN** | **DO OUR HOMEWORK** |

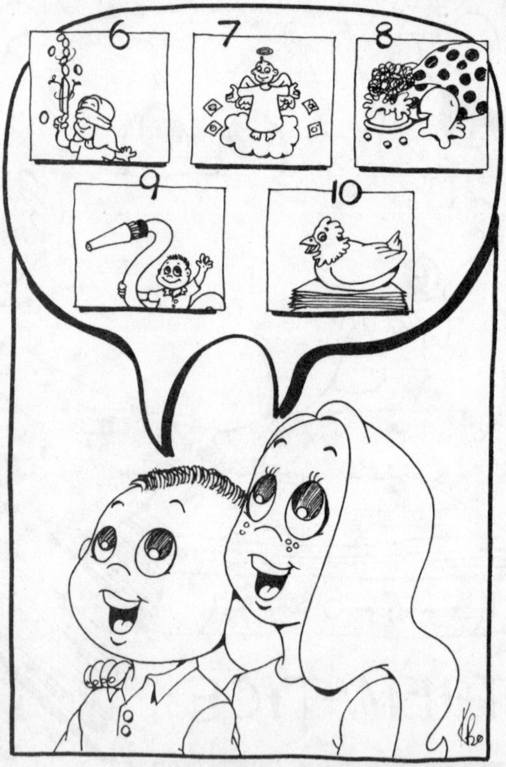


"That's great, kids! And you thought you couldn't remember things! As you can see, you each have an **excellent** memory," Grandpa laughed.

"Well, that's our ten silly stories," said Grandpa. "Let's go through our list from the beginning."

| | | |
|---|---|---|
| One | **DRUM** | **FEED THE CAT** |
| Two | **SHOE** | **PICK UP TOYS** |
| Three | **TREE** | **ICE-CREAM CONES** |
| Four | **DOOR** | **A BIG TOMATO** |
| Five | **HIVE** | **A CUSTARD PIE** |
| Six | **STICKS** | **A DOZEN EGGS** |
| Seven | **HEAVEN** | **HOLIDAY PHOTOS** |
| Eight | **GATE** | **CHOCOLATE CAKE** |
| Nine | **LINE** | **WATER THE GARDEN** |
| Ten | **HEN** | **DO YOUR HOMEWORK** |

Grandpa sat back in his chair and smiled.

"You see, you didn't have a problem with your memory. All you needed was a **way of remembering.** Each of you has an excellent memory."

"Grandpa, it's so easy. I'll never forget anything again," said Jasmine.

"Me either!" cried Adam.

HOME
SWEET
HOME

"Remember, **everyone** has a good memory, but you need a way to help you recall things.
And the way is **Memory Pegs** and **Silly Stories.**
And the **sillier** you make the stories the **easier** it is to remember your list."

"No one has a bad memory; people just don't know **how** to remember."

"Practise everyday and your memory will get better and better."

MEMORY PEGS
AND
SILLY STORIES!

"Thanks for helping us, Grandpa," said Adam. "We're going home now."

"It's time for tea."

"We love you, Grandpa, and we'll come over to see you on Sunday."

"And we **won't** forget."

As the children walked home they sang their new memory song:

This old man, he played **one**,
He played knick knack on my **drum**,
*With a knick knack paddy whack, give a dog a bone,*
*This old man came rolling home.*

This old man, he played **two,**
He played knick knack on my **shoe**,
*With a knick knack...etc.*

This old man, he played **three**,
He played knick knack on my **tree**,
*With a knick knack...etc.*

This old man, he played **four**,
He played knick knack on my **door**,
*With a knick knack...etc.*

This old man, he played **five**,
He played knick knack on my **hive**,
*With a knick knack...etc.*

This old man, he played **six**,
He played knick knack on my **sticks**,
*With a knick knack...etc.*

This old man, he played **seven**,
He played knick knack up to **heaven**,
*With a knick knack...etc.*

This old man, he played **eight**,
He played knick knack on my **gate**,
*With a knick knack...etc.*

This old man, he played **nine**,
He played knick knack on my **line**,
*With a knick knack...etc.*

This old man, he played **ten**,
He played knick knack on my **hen**,
*With a knick knack...etc.*

In the weeks that followed, Adam and Jasmine amazed their friends and family with their new way of remembering.

They could remember the whole weekly programme for the class, the entire recipe for a chocolate cake, the things that their Dad had to do at work and the names of ten of the headmaster's relatives!

They even won a prize for the highest marks in the school exams!

YOUR UNCLE'S NAME IS JOHN... HIS DAUGHTER IS SUSAN... HIS DOG IS FRED... HIS COUSIN...

And when they went shopping with their Mum she never ever needed a shopping list—the kids could remember everything!

Their teacher, Mrs Varney, was so impressed that she asked Adam and Jasmine if they would teach the class how to do it.

"Each of you has an excellent memory," the kids told the class. "But what you need is a **way** of remembering. First, let's start with a song that you'll all know..."

And so they all began to sing:

"This old man, he played **one,**
He played knick knack on my **drum,**
*With a knick knack paddy whack, give a dog a bone,*
*This old man came rolling home.*

This old man, he played **two**..."

WHAT YOU NEED IS A WAY OF REMEMBERING!

ONE IS DRUM
TWO IS SHOE
THREE IS TREE
FOUR IS DOOR
FIVE IS HIVE
SIX IS STICKS
SEVEN IS HEAVEN
EIGHT IS GATE
NINE IS LINE
TEN IS HEN

# *Advanced Section*

This section has exercises and tests to help you practise the memory peg system.

It also has several other techniques to show you how to remember groups of items and recall them in any order.

You'll be asked to write some of your own silly stories and to draw them so you'll need a pen or pencil from now on. We've given you plenty of space to practise your writing and drawing.

# *Exercise 1*

The teacher asks everyone to bring some items to school for a class project. She asks **you** to bring some:

1. ROCKS
2. SAND
3. HAIR
4. PAPERCLIPS
5. A TOOTHBRUSH

On the next pages, write or draw your own silly stories. To help you get started we've made up the first silly story and drawn the picture to show you how to do it.

Item One is ROCKS

ONE is DRUM

Pretend that you're in a band playing the drum but someone's filled it up with rocks and when you hit it, rocks fly out and hit the headmaster on the head!

BONK!!
OH NO!

Item Two is SAND

TWO is SHOE

Write or draw a silly story about sand and a shoe.

Item Three is HAIR

THREE is TREE

Write or draw a silly story about a tree and hair.

Item Four is PAPERCLIPS

FOUR is DOOR

Write or draw a silly story about paperclips and a door.

Item Five is a TOOTHBRUSH

FIVE is HIVE

Write or draw a silly story about a toothbrush and a hive.

# *Test Your Skills*

Write the memory peg for each number and then write the correct item

| Number | Memory Peg | Item |
|---|---|---|
| 1. | ________ | ________ |
| 2. | ________ | ________ |
| 3. | ________ | ________ |
| 4. | ________ | ________ |
| 5. | ________ | ________ |

Answers: 1. rock 2. sand 3. hair 4. paperclips 5. toothbrush.

# *Exercise 2*

## HOW TO PEG ALL FIVE ITEMS ON ONE NUMBER

Here's a way to expand your ability to remember large numbers of items.

Our five school items are:

1. rocks
2. sand
3. hair
4. paperclips
5. toothbrush

Now we'll make up a silly story about **all five items** and put them on memory peg number One which is DRUM.

You wake up in the morning and see that your hair is standing on end and there's a drum full of sand balancing on top of your hair and the sand is pouring all over you. You are wearing paperclips for earrings and each paperclip has a toothbrush hanging off it. Then a big rock comes out of the drum and dongs you on the head!

This method allows you to attach several items to each memory peg.

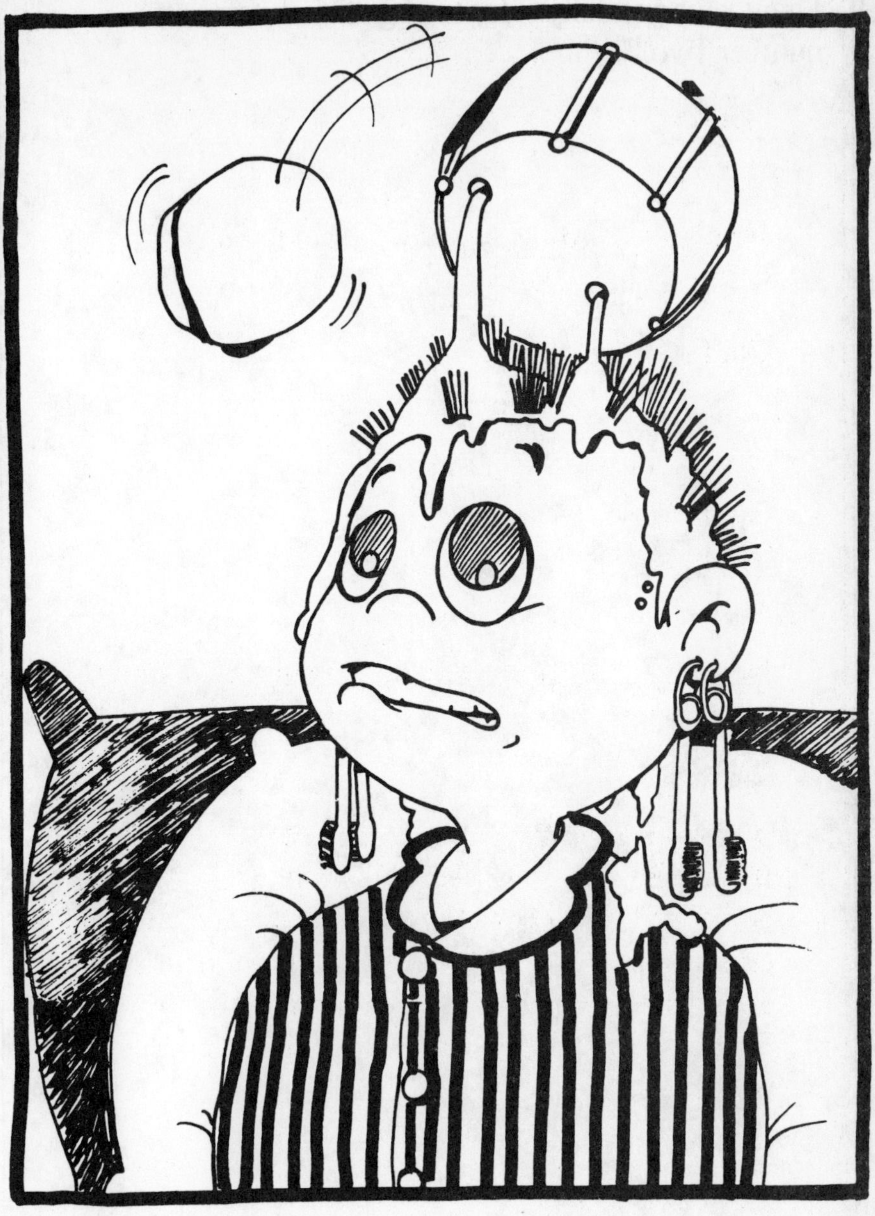

Draw your own silly story to peg all five items at number Two.

# *Exercise 3*

You have a school test tomorrow morning and you need to remember the names of five animals.

The animals are:

6. a kangaroo
7. a peacock
8. a crocodile
9. a horse
10. a pig

We'll do the first one for you and then you do the rest.

Item Six is a KANGAROO

SIX is STICKS

Imagine that you're in a forest and a kangaroo is trying to steal your stick. You're holding onto the stick as hard as you can but the kangaroo goes hopping off and takes you with him!

Item Seven is a PEACOCK

SEVEN is HEAVEN

Write or draw a silly story about a peacock in heaven.

Item Eight is a CROCODILE

EIGHT is GATE

Write or draw a silly story about a crocodile and a gate.

Item Nine is a HORSE

NINE is LINE

Write or draw a silly story about a horse and the line down the middle of the road.

Item Ten is a PIG

TEN is HEN

Write or draw a silly story about a hen and a pig.

# *Test Your Skills*

Write the memory peg for each number and then write the correct item

| Number | Memory Peg | Item |
|---|---|---|
| 6. | ________ | ________ |
| 7. | ________ | ________ |
| 8. | ________ | ________ |
| 9. | ________ | ________ |
| 10. | ________ | ________ |

Answers: 6. kangaroo 7. peacock 8. crocodile 9. horse 10. pig.

# *Test Your Skills*

Now let's write out both lists.

| SCHOOL LIST | ANIMAL LIST |
|---|---|
| 1. ________ | 6. ________ |
| 2. ________ | 7. ________ |
| 3. ________ | 8. ________ |
| 4. ________ | 9. ________ |
| 5. ________ | 10. ________ |

Answers: 1. rocks 2. sand 3. hair 4. paperclips 5. toothbrush
6. kangaroo 7. peacock 8. crocodile 9. horse 10. pig.

# *Exercise 4*

## REMEMBERING GROUPS OF ITEMS

Now think of **one** story involving **all** the five animals and peg them all at item number seven which is HEAVEN

Draw a silly story about heaven involving a kangaroo, a peacock, a crocodile, a horse and a pig.

# *Exercise 5*

Write the correct numbers next to each item.

| | |
|---|---|
| PAPERCLIPS | NUMBER ________ |
| PIG | NUMBER ________ |
| SAND | NUMBER ________ |
| HAIR | NUMBER ________ |
| KANGAROO | NUMBER ________ |
| ROCK | NUMBER ________ |
| HORSE | NUMBER ________ |
| CROCODILE | NUMBER ________ |
| TOOTHBRUSH | NUMBER ________ |
| PEACOCK | NUMBER ________ |

# *Exercise 6*

Write the correct item beside each of the following numbers.

| NUMBER | ITEM |
|---|---|
| 3 | ________________ |
| 5 | ________________ |
| 8 | ________________ |
| 1 | ________________ |
| 10 | ________________ |
| 7 | ________________ |
| 4 | ________________ |
| 9 | ________________ |
| 6 | ________________ |
| 2 | ________________ |

# *Exercise 7*

Now let's try a new list of ten different items. Five will be items that your Mum needs to do today and another five will be things that your Dad needs to remember.

Your Mum's five items are:

| | |
|---|---|
| 11. | pick up dry cleaning |
| 12. | get some bananas |
| 13. | post a letter |
| 14. | go to the bank |
| 15. | buy a lipstick |

Your Dad's list has these items:

| | |
|---|---|
| 16. | write a report |
| 17. | mow the lawn |
| 18. | fix oil leak in car |
| 19. | book a plane ticket to China |
| 20. | change a light bulb |

An easy way to recall these next ten items is to **join them** to the last ten items.

So here's how it would look:

| ORIGINAL LIST | | | NEW LIST |
|---|---|---|---|
| 1. DRUM | = ROCKS | + | 11. pick up dry cleaning |
| 2. SHOE | = SAND | + | 12. get some bananas |
| 3. TREE | = HAIR | + | 13. post a letter |
| 4. DOOR | = PAPERCLIPS | + | 14. go to the bank |
| 5. HIVE | = TOOTHBRUSH | + | 15. buy a lipstick |
| 6. STICK | = KANGAROO | + | 16. write a report |
| 7. HEAVEN | = PEACOCK | + | 17. mow the lawn |
| 8. GATE | = CROCODILE | + | 18. fix oil leak in car |
| 9. LINE | = HORSE | + | 19. book a plane ticket to China |
| 10. HEN | = PIG | + | 20. change a light bulb |

Let's start with item Eleven which is PICK UP THE DRY CLEANING. So now we join it to item One.

You'll recall that One is Drum = ROCKS.
Here's the silly story about the rocks.

To join the dry cleaning to the picture we add this extra bit.

"...the rocks hit the headmaster on the head. He falls backwards and his cup of coffee spills all over your Mum's dry cleaning."

Next is item Twelve which is GET SOME BANANAS..

Let's add it to item number Two.

Two is SHOE = SAND.

Now draw or describe your silly story about the shoe and the sand and then add some bananas to it.

Item Thirteen is POST A LETTER.

Now join it to the silly story in item Three.
So Three is TREE = HAIR + POST A LETTER
Make up a story about the tree, hair and a letter.

Item Fourteen is GO TO THE BANK.

Now make up a silly story about item Four which is DOOR and PAPERCLIPS and add the bank to the picture.

Item Fifteen is BUY A LIPSTICK.

Now join it to the silly story in item Five. So you have HIVE = TOOTHBRUSH + LIPSTICK.

# *Test your skills*

| FIRST LIST | NEW LIST |
|---|---|
| 1. ____________ | 11. ____________ |
| 2. ____________ | 12. ____________ |
| 3. ____________ | 13. ____________ |
| 4. ____________ | 14. ____________ |
| 5. ____________ | 15. ____________ |

Answers: 1. rocks 2. sand 3. hair 4. paperclips 5. toothbrush 11. pick up dry cleaning 12. bananas 13. post a letter 14 go to bank 15. buy a lipstick.

# *Exercise 8*

Now you have another five items to remember for your Dad.

You will need to peg them onto items Six, Seven, Eight, Nine and Ten.

| | | |
|---|---|---|
| Item | 16 | write a report |
| Item | 17 | mow the lawn |
| Item | 18 | fix oil leak in car |
| Item | 19 | book a plane ticket to China |
| Item | 20 | change a light bulb |

Item Sixteen is WRITE A REPORT.

Now join it to the silly story in item Six which is
STICKS = KANGAROO + REPORT.
Draw the picture.

Item Seventeen is MOW THE LAWN.

Now join it to the silly story in item Seven. So you have HEAVEN = PEACOCK + MOW THE LAWN.

Item Eighteen is FIX OIL LEAK IN CAR.

Now join it to the silly story in item Eight. So you have GATE = CROCODILE + FIX OIL LEAK IN CAR.

Item Nineteen is BOOK A PLANE TICKET TO CHINA.

Now join it to the silly story in item Nine. So you have LINE = HORSE + BOOK A PLANE TICKET TO CHINA.

Item Twenty is CHANGE A LIGHT BULB.

Now join it to the silly story in item Ten. So you have HEN = PIG + CHANGE A LIGHT BULB.

# *Test your Skills*

**FIRST LIST**

1. ____________
2. ____________
3. ____________
4. ____________
5. ____________
6. ____________
7. ____________
8. ____________
9. ____________
10. ____________

**NEW LIST**

11. ____________
12. ____________
13. ____________
14. ____________
15. ____________
16. ____________
17. ____________
18. ____________
19. ____________
20. ____________

Answers: 1. rocks 2. sand 3. hair 4. paperclips 5. toothbrush 6. kangaroo 7. peacock 8. crocodile 9. horse 10. pig 11. dry cleaning 12. bananas 13. post letter 14. go to bank 15. buy lipstick 16. write a report 17. mow lawn 18. fix oil leak in car 19. book plane ticket to China 20. change light bulb.

# *Exercise 9*

Now match the correct item with its right number.

| | | | |
|---|---|---|---|
| 13. | ________ | 10. | ________ |
| 2. | ________ | 3. | ________ |
| 11. | ________ | 16. | ________ |
| 18. | ________ | 5. | ________ |
| 19. | ________ | 8 | ________ |
| 6. | ________ | 12. | ________ |
| 4. | ________ | 1. | ________ |
| 20. | ________ | 14. | ________ |
| 15. | ________ | 7 | ________ |
| 9. | ________ | 17. | ________ |

Answers: see page 136.

# *Exercise 10*

Now put the correct numbers next to its right item.

| NO. | ITEM | NO. | ITEM |
|---|---|---|---|
| ___ | PAPERCLIPS | ___ | MOW LAWN |
| ___ | TOOTHBRUSH | ___ | PIG |
| ___ | GET BANANAS | ___ | SAND |
| ___ | GO TO BANK | ___ | HAIR |
| ___ | KANGAROO | ___ | PEACOCK |
| ___ | WRITE REPORT | ___ | ROCKS |
| ___ | DRY CLEANING | ___ | POST LETTER |
| ___ | BUY LIPSTICK | ___ | CROCODILE |
| ___ | BOOK TICKET TO CHINA | ___ | HORSE |
| ___ | FIX OIL LEAK IN CAR | ___ | MOW LAWN |
| ___ | CHANGE LIGHT BULB | ___ | WRITE REPORT |


Answers: see page 136.

FINALLY…

Here are some extra pages for you to practise writing and drawing your silly stories.

ONE IS DRUM
TWO IS SHOE
THREE IS TREE
FOUR IS DOOR
FIVE IS HIVE
SIX IS STICKS
SEVEN IS HEAVEN
EIGHT IS GATE
NINE IS LINE
TEN IS HEN